Breaking

New and selected poetry

Giles Dawnay

ISBN: 1729696090
ISBN-13: 978-1729696095

'Remember that sometimes
not getting what you want
is a wonderful
stroke of luck.'

Dalai Lama

Dedicated to Amy,
whose creativity and lightness of touch
is the real inspiration.

Contents

Role Models

Don't rush yourself
is what whispers
in the leaves of the
trees. Look what

can happen when
you take your time.
Nothing that can live
ever appeared over

night. The modern
world has brought
time to the immediate
and made us blind.

Be patient and take
your luck. And then
may the birds, of whom
you have no control,

settle in your wide
branches and sing
the glory of existence
held fast by solid roots.

Sunset at the Beach

Soft sand welcomes home each hard
footstep. To move forward is to allow
small embrace. An evening couple,
with gentle gait and easy smiles
roll on by, panting life as they go.

Fading light as the breakers roar.
Row after row of dusky white teeth,
smiling ambiguously to the shore.
Without colour the body becomes the eye,
feeling the great ocean, the soul quivers.

Retracing my steps to return, already
they are washed away. There is no
backwards, only new and forwards.
When memory surrenders. I am here,
for the first time, over and over again.

Cartography

Man makes the maps
but the territories, well,
they make themselves.

Land changes, maps
get sold and stay still.
How to capture something
which is always moving.

Think of a person
as their own beach.
The waves break
on the moving sandbar,
or calcified reef
that lies beneath.
It's power and expression
depending on storms
that cannot be seen,
depending on tides
that cannot be controlled.

Who do I meet,
when I meet someone else?
For I am changing
and so are they.

Always.

Seasons

That's just not my mum,
he whispers, soft dark eyes
looking ahead and behind
into another time and space.

Outside the trees stand bare,
skeletal fingers gracefully twist,
spiral and dance to a naked sky.
A small crinkle of leaves at their roots.

She sits, eyes closed, resting
as an oxygen mask rasps
its gifts into her failing lungs.
A hard crag sits above her nipple.

The land softens and muddies
with the falling of the rain,
the baked hardness of summer gone
and the world less sure underfoot.

It's funny, he offers, I normally help
tidy their houses after they've gone,
being an estate agent and all.
Before his words fade back to silence.

Pale sunshine lights up the day,
branches clack and click with
the passing of the breeze, winter
wears a different coat to summer.

She did love a cigarette, he exhales,
breathing into a tangled web of feeling.
The elements pitter-patter gently on the window,
singing softly the advent of another season.

Explosions

No matter who is speaking,
someone
must have
the last word.

No matter the subject,
someone
must have
the first word.

In the beginning was the Word,
and the word made flesh.
In the beginning was the Big Bang,
and sound led to form.

So much of our brief lives
we define through noise.
Who are any of us
when reduced to silence?

But then who are any of us
when all we can do is talk,
and what does it mean
to not know how to listen?

They Know

They know they do,
when to grow
how to be,
when to slow.

That's how they became
their great frame
standing tall
yet to fall.

Using the season
as their guiding reason
dropping their leafy cloak
in a cloud of golden smoke.

They don't hang on
to last summer's song,
knowing the right time,
and stillness is no crime.

For they are their roots
that no one sees,
deep in the rich earth
that makes them trees.

They are who they are
by having ventured in,
shivering in denuded elegance,
while their human cousins
rage on, trying to win.

House Rules

Throw open the windows,
pull back the curtains. No
house can breathe unless
it can exchange its air.

Ghosts prosper where change
does not. Rotting corpses
fester in cobwebbed rooms
where vibrant feasts once raged.

To live, a house must expire
as much as it inspires. It must
move with the seasons, accept
all guests lovingly when they come,

and let them go when the clock strikes
farewell. Rivers that cannot flow
soon poison all who come near. How
ravenously disease feasts on stale air.

Eternity smiles knowing all hard-won
walls must fall as time and water
have their way. Leaving only memory
of space and how it was used to those left,
still in the process of building their own.

Bricks and Mortar

To go away, is
to come back.

Take what you
need, and no
more. Maybe

it is in staying
put, that clutter
begins to thrive.

Where is it
that we live?

Bricks and mortar
or heart and mind?

Precious choice
never far from home.

Stabbed in January

Who are you?
Can we get access please.

Why are you here?
Major haemorrhage call please.

Who wanted to kill you?
What's his Blood Pressure?

How did your life take you here?
Theatre is ready.

Who gave birth to you?
He's a drug user, veins collapsed.

What did the drugs protect you from?
Can't get access.

How did your life become so cheap?
He's got Hep C be careful.

What type of life must you have had?
Blood going in, squeeze that bag.

Do you even want to live?
Theatres have called, let's move

Holy Day

A holiday, a holy day,
where time is precious
and there can be rest
from the daily bread.

But then, is every day
not holy? Every day
another chance given
to find God in the nooks

and crannies of the sweaty
concrete embalming the walls
of civilization. What
is this time away, if it means

that daily life remains bereft?
Otherwise does not the
laughter and happiness found
in the glorious golden beaches

and deep infinite mountains
echo mockingly in the corners
of the mind's chamber? The deceit
that God awaits, but not here.

Desert Fire

Come into the wilderness,
Your voice calls from within.
For there is nothing to fear
and I shall meet you here.

For while we meet endlessly
in the joy and laughter
of all that you share with others,
you can never know Me

until we have danced madly
and sung wildly in the desert
alone with no more than
the stars to lighten our steps.

And love will forever be
out of reach until you
truly have witnessed
where I am.

Sunrise (NHS Baby Checks)

I came to check your baby
to make sure all was correct,
my role that day to make sure
the appropriate data to collect.

But instead you invited me in
to the dark womb of where you sat,
to put down my clipboard and questions
and take off my clinician's hat.

For to you as a new mother
there was nothing better than to look,
to stare into this squirming mystery
who could never be explained by any book.

For what seemed a time eternal
we both gazed at this new life,
not needing to find answers
or wield analysis' deadly knife.

Three of us in that fertile cubicle,
perhaps all of us having been born.
All suspended in an ocean of wonder,
intellects heavy veil thankfully torn.

This moment a great reminder
that while the work must be done,
what is it all for, if we keep
missing the rising of the sun?

They Know Not What

Nailed to the cross
bleeding out
slowly
to a baying
crowd.

Physical death
not enough but
social identity too,
ripped mercilessly
to shreds.

Total destruction of the external, creating life-giving access to the eternal. His message clear, this is what you must do.

Yet still the crowd bray,
now wearing his livery.
Demanding yet more
crucifixions
for those
endangered souls
lost on the way.

Earnestly preparing
more ornate crosses
for those
dammed others.
Deemed to be
in desperate
need of eternal
salvation.

Musicality

I am music,
part of the universal
orchestra.

My notes vibrate out
into the great sound,
finding harmony
when I listen,
and discord
when too loud.

Played by the breath
of life, that I cannot own
but can only allow
to let sing from
the nurtured instrument
of my being.

Playing to a conductor
that no one sees
but that lives deep
in the beat of all rhythm,
even when out of time.
Playing together
but not always as one,
we practice on.

We are all music,
breathlessly awaiting
the next chorus
where both we, and
eternity's melody,
drop back into
mutual symphony.

Slumber

To start again
maybe nothing
more than to
close your eyes.

Then the moment
you can feel both
body and breath,
let them open again.

Light and love
will be awaiting,
just as they were
when you last awoke.

Backs to the future

Imagine a world where
those who walk do so
ambling forwards
facing backwards.

With eyes strained and fixed
on a horizon that spins away.
Focused on the setting sun,
colourful as is its design,
than looking breathlessly ahead
wondering what may come
as the light begins to fade.

What of the brave flowers,
that each day fling open
the petals of safety
and let light and life
find them as they are.
Do they only think
of what was?

And what of Christ,
who showed us that to go
beyond, we must open
our arms and allow them
to be nailed wide.
Eternity remains
in the unseen shadows,
hidden by the crosses
that we all refuse
to know as our own.

Taxonomy

Gold is gold
whether we label
it that or not.

Good is good
whether seen
or unwitnessed.

And God is God.
Existing far beyond
the infinite names

of right and wrong,
we spend so long
falling out over.

Gospel Pass, Hay on Wye

Up high, swimming in the blues and greens,
land, sky and cloud all scudding towards
an elusive horizon. Passers-through sit
and stare, attempting to understand where
it is they sit. How to capture such space,

a question that technology can never
quite answer. Nothing noisier than
the gentle friction of breeze skimming
through the valley, all other noise internal
as we rest and gaze. A lost sheep, shorn

and wild breaks the peace, running and
yelling for all its worth. None of its kind
offer a reply, too busy eating. Eventually
it stops to look before hurtling on. What
secrets his language hides can only

be guessed. Perhaps lost, perhaps mad,
perhaps even singing. Perhaps he feels
the drums of troubles to come. Maybe
even, his plight is no different to the rest
of us. How best to live in all this space?

Hibernus

White soft snow falling
on the grey hard road.
No time to settle as it does
like a soothing blanket
over the gentle sleeping
green giants that slumber
rising up above the hedgerows.

The earth and clay know
no rush, not for them
to impatiently beep, honk
or tailgate those roots
that are venturing ever deeper.

Happy to let this pure shroud
be thrown over this wintery rigor mortis.
The sacred sheet offering
redemption to what lies beneath
now hidden from unseeing eyes.

While those in mobile metal coffins
rush, here, there and everywhere.
Frantic to make sure that they
have fully lived before the soft
ground welcomes them home.

Taking the bait

I wonder if they know who is watching,
THE great hunter of the sea, as it rockets
from the murky deep, to take fake bait.
A tight ball of enormous silver muscle,
dark eyes and endless teethy ridges.
Millions of years honing evolution.

Does it know we watch, laughing in terror,
locked in clever cages. The zoo reversed.
Nature's greatest killer finally behind bars.
Before gone, diving down back to the depths
of its world and our imagination. What
of the electric pulse felt of our hearts,
the strange chemical residue we leave.

Do they then go back to their own journey
daring to consider that beyond their realm
there is more they do not know? Or like us,
is the act of living so overwhelming that
having got what they need, instinct and
desire simply fixes on the next consumption.

Saturn's Return

Saturn's spinning and returning,
ringing its way back to where
it was 27 years ago. A time,

so they say, for the clock
to restart and a chance
for rebirth, to love again.

You are 27 and you lie
before us. A broken artery
bleeds into soft brain.

New Year's Eve, you planned
of children to come, four
days later you are dead.

Saturn has returned for all
of us who met you. Rebirth
screaming loudly in the
corridors of our souls.

Sprung

Bright yellow buttercups like lovers, lounging
side by side on plush blades of green,
faces to the sun, opening their leaves
of love and laughter to the open air.

Sparkles of daisies scattered amongst,
like far off stars springing from the moist earth,
a floral universe laid out on this vibrant veneer,
beseeching us to gaze, but offering little clue

as to how or why the mesmerising way
this wild life appears the way it does.
The gentle Wye lumbers alongside,
as though a thick and muscular artery,

it too moves life in front of our eyes, from
somewhere we cannot see to another
place we might never know. Perhaps some
of that water will come to us, perhaps

some of our water will end up there?
I stand, facing up the stream, a bright
galaxy to my right, pulsing vitality to
to my left and the blinding sun in my eyes.

For the briefest of eternal moments, I can
no longer feel my edges, these boundaries
I so often desire to protect. There is only
existence, and I belong to no one and no thing.

But instead, held inside this passing form
that too has so momentarily sprung, swaying
in the cool breeze, my naked toes gripping the
damp clay.
                                        Forever somewhere,
lost and found between the mysteriousness
of the infinite galaxies and the ever-flowing
endlessness of life-giving water.

Eloi, eloi

Curiously named this Good Friday.
The day mankind turned their backs
on One who had come to their need.

Yet we persist calling it Good.
Perhaps to spare the shame
of refusing to see yet again

in whom and where God exists.
As we continue, hell bent,
crucifying everything but ourselves
in the name of seeking paradise.

Change

She comes,
the great teacher,
whose face no one
has ever seen.

Walking at her own pace
through the busy street,
unannounced yet, in truth,
expected by us all.

Never wearing
the same clothes
and singing her lessons
always in a different key.

We are invited to come
like children, and sit
where her endless robes
billow against the dust.

There might we listen
to what she has to say,
not always understanding or
knowing when she will come again.

Before we stand up once more
and return to private worlds,
Places that now no longer resemble
the ones from which
we were called.

White Out

Padding through the fresh white
that has now settled, incubating all
beneath in an apparent soft purity.

It almost feels a crime to leave
ragged tracks, broken and scraggy
across a landscape that is dressed

as one ready for her wedding day.
The smoothness of her contours
and softness reminds of a new-born,

whose soft canvas is yet to be
written on, or even trampled.
But we are here too, and our footprint

no less natural than the fluttering flakes.
What perhaps separates us, choice
of where our own feet might fall, and
how lightly we may choose to walk.

Puddle Reflections for the under 3's

I just want to stand in puddles,
the big grey sloshy ones,
the ones where I can see
someone like me smiling back
standing on the other side.

I want to jump, feel the wetness
make my purple trousers wet,
make my toes slimy. I want to
jump and splash, and make
the water jump too. What else

is there to do? The big people
like to stand and talk, I can't always
understand what they murmur but
they never jump in puddles. Only me
and my friend who always smiles back.

They always want to be somewhere
else, so I never have long to jump
in puddles. They say it is better over
there, but I don't see any puddles.
Best to keep jumping all day long!

Sirens of Eden

They sing, sweetly and innocently,
the Sirens of the past, from the island
of yesterday, where the sun shines
and abundant crops grow. They call

to all who dare sail near, to abandon
the unknown ocean ahead and return
to a familiar land that become more detailed
with the passing of time. They promise

in their gentle and mellifluous shanties,
a better place where chaos has order
and uncertainty is understood. Pain
of the past, easily forgotten in the present.

Yet what they do not sing, no traveller
will find them despite valiant efforts.
Hidden rocks will dash their creaking ships
again and again, leaving them marooned

to sink under a blazing sun, as other vessels
sail on to the horizon. The Sirens will keep
singing regardless, knowing they too cannot
live, unless they are continued to be sought.

Timed out

Late again, too busy lost admiring
the autumnal dappled light spraying
against flaming leaves that turn to leave.

An empty blue sky, paling towards
darker and shorter days, deathly winter
must come and there is little choice

but to graciously accept. But I am
still late, regardless this natural wonder.
Despite all worthy protestations I belong

to a human world too. Whose materialism
is as petty as grimy flotsam cast adrift
at sea, yet whose inner world is as wild

and expansive as the pulsing universe.
Time clunks scalding our eyes. How to live
in both worlds, today's repeating question.

Sound Waves

I was doing so well on my island,
and then the music happened,
and before I knew the bamboo hut
of my mind collapsed into the water
the tidal wave took me from the beach
and my body became held in sound.

The rainbow of vibration swept me
from the dry world of sandy word
to the flowing sea of wet, wordless emotion.
And we swam, ducked and dived.
I did not know where I was
or how long I would be there for.

Until the music finished and the waves
returned me, left again with only my words,
ragged and washed up on the shore.
Gasping for breath yet ecstatic,
wondering how long it would be
until I might be snatched up
and forced to gloriously swim again.

DIY

Build your house
and by all means
make it strong.

But when the time
comes, to sit in
your porch taking rest;

take time to look out
rather than proudly in.
And see how all that

grows from the ground
knows nothing of rigidity
or perfect stillness,

but moves beautifully
in time, with the passing
of each season.

Appraisal

Today he died
but she lived.
Ask me what
sort of day
I have had
and there are
no words.

All I know
is that I
was a witness,
but that my day
came and went.

And how can
I even begin
to complain if
I had the privilege
to be the observer
rather than the
unfortunately
observed.

Lost in Translation

Speak to me of words
and there is confusion.
That glass jar, it is easy,
there are molecules trapped
in the form of jar and glass.

But tell me of a river, and
what are we saying?
The static word cannot
describe something that
flows, and keeps flowing.
Of what structure do we talk?

How to talk about something
that isn't only one some thing?
No wonder illusion abounds.
Imagine applying the same logic
to a living being.

Then step back,
and bow our minds and hearts.
We are in the presence of mystery.

Half Way Here

I've lived half my life,
I heard someone say.
How did he know?
I heard myself wonder.

The statistics might say
it is true, but uncertainty
tells me that none of us
really know what will

happen later on today.
At any moment then, have
we not lived all our life?
If so,
            what does that mean?

Eco illogical

Perhaps those Greeks knew something
we didn't, cleverly calling the environment
the 'oikos.' They saw everywhere as home.

Not just the small temporal constructs where
they laid their nightly heads. I wonder what
they would think of such things now as grandly

called 'eco-homes.' Would they sit curiously
and listen to the modern understanding, or
just look on in quiet disbelief, like a parent who
has seen their child drunk for the first time.

Ten minutes

Next patient in, I wonder who will come.
The list only short as I am in training. Always
curious to see people's reaction to the length
of time it takes to train, as though life will
be better when it is all done. I am not
convinced. Those higher up the power chain
rarely look like life is better. Simply older.

He doesn't speak any English and his family
are with him. He wants to be seen downstairs
as he can't make it up. I am not sure I am
ready for this. His notes give little away,
but that he is a refugee, he has cancer,
he doesn't speak much English, he arrived
here recently. I sit in my own thoughts,

I have been struggling for meaning in my
own life recently. What am I doing, how
am I spending my time? What of my own
potential. Today gratitude and I dance
the dance of ex-lovers condemned to be
awkward strangers. He walks in, a soft manner
floating above physical heaviness. His wife,
all smiles and headdress accompanies. So do
three children with bright eyes and open faces.

No one has any clue what to do, 'leeettle eeenglish.'
He apologies but it is me that feels inadequate.
Locked in this man is story and need, only
language can help me access. Google translate
on a screen lets us begin. He has rectal cancer,
he can no longer control his bowels, he needs
incontinence pads. I must change, two
to three time a day. He types this onto the
dispassionate screen. What does this man

have left I wonder. He has no option but
to write openly, his family witnessing
his physical frailty without any hashtag filter.
his shoulder is almost useless, google translates
his Arabic words to 'shrapnel…explosion.'
A phone translator connects us a little closer,
he needs a sick note to claim help. Still nothing
is completely clear.

Finally, a hurried lady
from Refugee International is contacted.
I can speak freely again, initially rough
she softens on learning I am his doctor, not
a receptionist. He needs a repeat sick note,
we have been here for almost forty-five.
This consultation could have taken 10 minutes.
As a country we can provide this help to
those to whom vicissitude has taken so much.
A meaner voice, whose origin is uncertain
reminds me again in very certain terms.
This consultation could have taken 10 minutes.

But it didn't and I am glad. I have been granted
extended company with the type of life
I might never know. I am not sure who
has been the doctor and who the patient
as they walk out the door. But I, for one,
find it hard to feel the same emptiness I did
when his name first appeared on my screen.

Spinning

Concrete arteries pumping
metallic blood cells, human
oxygen sitting inside, driving
their madcap evolution forward.

The air crisp, ruddy red leaves
suspended in the golden glow
of the kneeling sun, blazingly bowing
to the unrepentant goddess Change.

In a far off jungle a leathery man
and velvet jaguar stare hungrily
at each other's eyes. Neither sure
to trust in instinct or thought.

Here, a new bride, all in white, sits as
all she has ever wanted now presses
heavy on her delicate chest. Accepting
love, one of the hardest human steps.

A whir of blue and green, suspended
in darkness. This life given by one star
of many. Yet how to live, perhaps always
to be unanswered, in the unseen silence.

Long Division

The world around me changed
but the atoms did not.

The seasons came and went,
skeletal tress exploded to soft blossom,
hard bark to life-giving green,
grey slate skies to bright vibrant blues.
Rain transformed from cold and harsh
to sublime warm and embracing.
And back again.

But the atoms, they stayed the same.
All they did was move and dance
from one form to the next.

People exploded into being, burning
brightly but not always avoiding
the black holes left by some others
that hungrily devour the careless.
But the atoms, they just moved on.

Time ticked, in the clock that must
one day break down. But in the echo
of each click, lies an unwitnessed eternity.
Hiding in the day-to-day objects,
waiting for us to carefully look again.

Static

Stay still for a second,
nothing seems to move.

Stay still for a minute
and see the tree
branch delicately twitch
in an unseen breeze.

Stay still for an hour
and follow the clouds
as they scud across
a sky that is more than blue.

Stay still for a day,
and watch the light come
and go, seamlessly
merging with darkness.

Stay still for a year
and watch the colours of
the earth rise and fall
like waves in a thudding ocean.

Stay still for eternity
and witness that change
is all there is. From the furthest
reach of the universe
to the four chambers of your heart.

Stay still once more for a second,
and feel you heart beat
and your chest rise and fall.
Why isn't that enough?

Promises

The flower grows
by being still.
Opening delicate petals
to the light and bees,
as it must, to fulfil
its own promise.

The tree grows
by being still.
Opening strong branches
to the light and animals,
as it must, to fulfil
its own promise.

We too grow
when in stillness.
Allowing us to
fling open our arms

and reveal
a soft, beating heart
to the divine light
and all other beings,
that seek to make
us their home.

Anointing day

And so they gather, in the hushed room.
A man in white robes takes the lead,
reading from the reprinted texts that
have been passed down from those
before. He stands, we stand. He sits, we sit.

Words spring forth, the assembled
add their low tones to give them life.
Some who stand can always be heard,
others lips move, without sound, unsure
in the battle of authenticity and belief.

In the centre, still blinded by the light,
a newer human, dressed too in white robes.
For now she must be carried to each new
destination by those who feel they must
do the best for her. Today she is here

even though here for her is still
everywhere. Water pours across her brow
and she keeps her own water inside.
How well behaved the gathered few
jokingly agree. Laughter finally flows.

Back in her basket, this little one still yet
to differentiate the energy around her in
which she swims, looks into the light.
The early path of her life which she will
be taken begins to emerge for those who carry.

The challenge of her own life now begun.
Traditional creed versus personal experiences
of reality. Is it better to be given nothing
and walk into life with no guidance,
or start with the unmet truth of another?

All of us squinting into the glare, trying
to make sense of the shapes. All of us
spending our lives trying to find home,
perhaps as many ways to get there as
pairs of eyes adjusting to the light.

Solar Defibrillation

Filling time can
be to lose time.
To seek productivity can

be the murder of creativity.
To fear annihilation is
perhaps to be dead already.

Paradox creeps at every corner
of a world crudely constructed
to make sense of existence.

Too easy to be haunted
by the ghosts of previous selves,
that now exist only in the stories

when I forget to be still.
Feeling the sun on my face,
and letting that be enough.

Sledging

A flash of hard yellow and soft curl,
screaming with speed and laughter
the little one flies down the snowy mountain,
no fear for her in this whitened land.

Looking back there are dark shadows
on the hill, arms raised and whooping,
celebrating her youth. Excited words said
about fearlessness and courage.

Hard not to see youth and think of ones
own, now seemingly lost to memory and story.
To think of the twists, turns and possibility
that was once there. When a sledge

was the ultimate in adventure and daredevilry.
Yet now the body creeks and the ground too
far away to simply hurl oneself towards.
Yet perhaps, this is all just more yarn

told to keep ourselves away and safe
from the terrifying truth we hide well. These
moments of wild abandon don't have to end,
it is only the stories that stop them.

Connective Tissue

Next time your passion
sends you down
deep into the darkness.

Ask yourself from where
does originate this drive?
If the answer whispers

I just want to be loved,
then stop and take a breath.
When you open your

eyes again, look around.
And then welcome yourself
back to the human race.

Space

In the temple
that was built,
but not in the bricks.
He is there.

In the music
that was played,
but not in the written note,
She is there.

In the apparent distance
between me and you,
but not in the thoughts.
It is there.

For God lives,
both hidden
in what we can see,
and dancing freely
in the unseen spaces.

Waiting patiently
for all that is solid
to lovingly return.

Breakfast of the prodigal

An empty charred kettle reminds me
of what I do not have. How many
roaring cups of tea have come,
how much laughter has been shared
from its twisted and gnarled spout?

With no one to talk with, my mind chats.
Asking questions, solving problems,
swirling and whirling its neural carousel.
To sit alone feels like an act of rebellion,
defying the unnamed lust for stimulation.

In silence my body aches, deep to its core,
a longing to share. In the quiet creeps
another sound, an unseen orchestra of birdsong.
Gentle tumblings of a nearby waterfall
the tender rub of breeze on green shoots.

Heavy clouds buffet the dark hills, bright
light peaks through the mantles cracks
making me squint. You are as alone,
the silence speaks, as you choose to be.
Come and play, you have never left home.

Blinded

When the world is dark
and the eyes cannot see.
Rejoice, for you are close,
close to all what you seek.

It is not dark because you are
lost, but the obscurity is one
of the mind, and its inability
to understand what it sees.

There is no man-made torch
to take you further, but instead
your divine inheritance of love,
which too often lays discarded.

For love never asks to know.
Instead it simply yearns to feel.
And in this leap of faith,
promises safe passage through

to the true light that exists.
Hidden deep in all things
but forever burning,
blindingly bright.

Rainbow Nation

Hot coffee on the white verandah,
a black man in indigo overalls
wanders past, holding his slate
grey ladder. Pretty children all

dressed in pink, laugh and giggle
in this green gardened world, pale
reddened mothers nod to one another,
an invisible husband can provide

only so much. Table Mountain looms
over this shared thread. An empty
but electric blue sky holds the unseen air,
free to all in its blows and buffets.

Clean white cars hold the hot asphalt,
dazzling white smiles wait on the curb,
dark thumbs pointed upwards hoping
the day's work will come. Up above

the drone of another heavy metal bird
that comes to bring and take. Yellow
and orange fills sky and ocean, the day
takes it bow to all, before a violet darkness
again seeps in to briefly wash all colour away.

Look before you leap

I see a clear river
flowing softly
over bed and rocks.

I want to dive in
but for a moment
have to stop,

how can I be so sure?
It looks deep
but water distorts.

I think of the stories
upon which my life
is precariously built.

I want truth,
I want to understand,
but memory distorts

the light by which I see.
So instead I decide to sit,
lowering myself in gently.

Turned out the river
was not as deep as it seemed,
but I did enjoy the swim.

RSVP BYO

Beware that dammed drinks party
of the minds ambitions.
Huddled together you jostle
chinking fizzy glasses
and passing ornate canapés
with those wonderful desires.

Where despite welcoming them
and asking how they are,
you still can't help but look
insouciant over their shoulder
to the next sparkling guest
you itch to come your way.

Lottery Tickets

Yesterday I met
a two-day year old
girl whose mother
was not allowed
to be near her.

You see, her mother
had injected all sorts
of drugs as the baby
grew inside of her
and her father was
currently in prison.

This two-day old
looked like the other
little babies she shared
her space with. Yet
she was being given
morphine, to help her
go *cold turkey* too.

What does life hold
now for her, was
our unspoken thought.
Will pain give birth
to pain, or will love
find a way to forgive?

Next time any of us feel
how hard forgiveness
is, perhaps spare a
thought, for how tough
it could have been.

Children's Hour

It's all very well
calling ourselves
children of God

but then using
that as an excuse
not to grow up.

By all means
stay humble.
But please

don't let any
clever wording
stop you

from embracing
your divine gifts,
and taking full

responsibility for
every single little
thing that you do.

Autumns Apples

Imagine falling, when no one
even knew you grew. Scattered
amongst the many, just another
that reached potential but then

dropped. The surrounding elders,
changing their heavy green cloak to
golden tweed of molten fire and lava.
For them too, the season of plenty
draws in, the tide of darkness encroaches
ever higher on their thick, rugged shore.

So many fallen, so many unknown.
Circumstance and location the only
reason as to who gets picked and
who must return their form. Quiet,
unseen, no fanfare to their departing.

To become, yet not be seen. How then
to find peace as strong bodies melt
unwitnessed into a soily cauldron? Maybe
the final act of faith. To believe a fulfilled
but silent life still leaves the earth enriched.

Twisted Crux

Untwist the cross of your own life,
open your branches wide
and stand fully facing both the sun
and storm in equal measure.

Your life will be defined not
by what the public reward
but by your capacity
to embrace the suffering.

And if you can make a friend
in the pain of not knowing,
then can you too, dancing gently
like the light of the morning sun

breathing life into the shadows
of the fallen night, and breathing
beauty and love into the other
twisted silhouettes who carry
but still deny their own mortal cross.

Fidgeting

At some point,
no matter who
we are or what
we do, we must

return to sit alone
in our own room.
And for all our success
and reward from outside,

what does any of it mean
if, upon becoming silent,
our first grand reaction is to
reject the arrival of stillness?

British Umpire

Back to the crease again,
men in white who have hibernated
the long winter finally set free.

The grassy knolls and spaces are set,
the carefully tended to arena is glorious, as though
the dream of the British Empire made real.
This is how life could be, with dazzling uniforms
against vibrate green and hopeful blue.

There are rules, but only designed to bring
beauty to chaos. There is etiquette and
a sense of decency, how to be and treat
fellow man and competitor.

Each man
part of a team but also deeply individual,
knowing that to win means joining in
but also standing up when it is time
to be counted.

No one wants to lose, but winning must
be done with stealth, the ultimate in
ungentlemanly behaviour would be
to be caught on the boundary of
naked competition. No, true winning
must happen *only* as a by-product
of playing up and playing the game.
Otherwise it will be worth nothing,
and the men in flannels know this.

Mother nature watches on, her children
doing her proud. Confused as to which
imaginary game they have concocted
on this occasion and why in this land
such a game has been invented that
requires endless supply of good weather.
Yet she applauds imagination and endeavour,
in her offspring, simply happy her progeny
are not somewhere else causing trouble.

Shouts and enthusiasm filter into the
warm summer air. The birds in their hidden
wisdom tweet back vociferously,
nearby trees softly rattle their branches.
The sky stretches its wide azure arms,
scored with white smoky trails and
the occasional cloud, lost and out of
season. In a universe where the axioms
are unclear, it is these rules that bring
temporary order to chaos. And for a blink
of eternities eyelid, it is glorious.

School Run

Mummies and Daddies,
well, mainly mummies,
emerging from soft beds
into hard routines.

Little ones, on the path
to become bigger ones,
dressed in odd fitting clothes
designed to make them the same
although bigger people love
telling them they are different.

The crucible of the playground
awaits, the shrieking melting pot
of hopes, dreams and ice creams.
Sweets, treats and car seats
left at home for another day.

A blue painted line razors across the tarmac,
big people on one side, little ones
on the other. A stray parent
wanders across in a haze of love
and protection. Another, whose face
is as tight as their gym wear,
crunches an expression of disapproval.

Bells go and clocks tick. The world
of lines awaits. Little ones
now becoming their own line.
Stand straight, drink your water.
Commands slosh from the watching mob.

And in the silence, once all
standing here have departed,
the blue line rests. Just another
splash of colour until order's
imagination makes it real,
dividing again those who see it.

The Ride

You know when it's coming
when the restless blue darkens
beginning to offer up gifts
of sparkling diamonds to the sky.

Rising up, a watery mountain
thunders ever closer, roaring
deep from the ocean jungle.
Move or be moved, she calls.

And then the cliff face.
Where used to be gently flat,
now the terrifying potential
of space, and how to use it.

Before, if Neptune approves,
brief ticket to a world where
water is solid, countless soft
green fingers raise themselves,

holding their empty passenger
in a grip of feathered violence.
Until it is over, the pulsing deep
remembering itself and its rules.

The ones who forgot themselves
in order to travel beyond,
now no more than just another
set of dark bobbing indistinct heads.

But in those heads and hidden
bodies lie a certainty imprinted
by a present moment gone too
fast. Those ecstatic hearts

that now beat with renewed
purpose, know without doubt
that the world of sight offers
but a paltry lit, flickering candle.

When placed in steep contrast
to the visceral drop into
to the kingdom of feeling, where
God awaits, all those who let go.

Half in, half out

There's a rotting badger lying there
up on the hill, half flattened
half bulbous, its death odour
leaks out from where it lies.

Its slain corpse, a sacrifice
to our self-important progress.
Body half on concrete, half
in the wet hedge, no need
to explain this symbol.

Collateral damage in the quest
to dominate our changing nest,
Our animal neighbours yet
to truly appreciate the low interest
finance package, latest speeding cars.

No doubt somewhere, someone
is begrudgingly paying to have
a car dent fixed, bemoaning
how stupid the wildlife is.

All the while this little fellow
who knew no better, slowly
returns to where he started.
While we all drive ever faster

to avoid the chasing thought
that we too, might one day fall,
agonisingly culled somewhere
between the green life-giving verge
and the grey decaying road.

Small steps

If every moment in your life
seems to have prepared you
for a later moment,

then fear not. This very same
moment, that right now
only resembles chaos,

will one day be lovingly
looked back on. As yet
another vital step.

Rhossili Cemetery

Dead fish strewn on an open sandy grave,
mouths open and eyes gone, their spirits
long since swum. Empty rotting carcasses
that roll and spin on the white petticoat
of the dancing tide and her nimble steps.

All the same size and all with eyes and mouths
looking hauntingly beyond. How could it be
that so many have been chosen to make
these golden gravels their place for sky burial?
The smell of death lingers in the fresh air,
children fly kites and scream with salty delight
as mother ocean embrace their small bodies.

Their lives, still to be played out. And these days,
some that they may remember as some of the best
of a childhood now long gone. When life was
simply there to play, for as long as possible.
Decisions could be made by others who knew
what to do. But these grey and fetid fish

remain as cairns for a world into which this youth
must climb. Monuments to the sins of all our fathers,
for whom exploitation has replaced play as a means
to live. Too small for the industrial catch, so thrown
back in by scaly men who too have families to feed.

Oh for the days when there was nothing more
than sandwiches, kites and crisps on Eden's beach.
What responsibility we all have, to look after
our own but also our brother and sister earthly spirits.
And what have we become if, in such killing, we can
easily discard all that does not meet the bottom line.

Shop, skip and jump

Loud music thumps
against the temples from
where they have risen from.

Bright lights and red signs
yelling everything is for sale.
Drunk on choice, homo sapiens

remains hunted, unable to decide
what it really needs or
where it should go next.

Once solitude is no longer welcome
loneliness will stalk its prey,
cunningly and without noise

hidden in the foliage
of any untended to
life-giving silence.

Safari

One man set out on the journey of his destiny,
driven on by the flames of internal desire.
He refused all help that came his way,
ceaseless in his movement but never arriving.
His destination remained beyond the shimmering horizon.

Another man set out on the journey of his destiny
driven on by the invisible trade winds that filled his sails.
Welcoming all help and refuge that came his way.
Until he arrived at his destination, even while still moving.
And the journey stopped being only his,
but everyone's.

Paradise

'then you'll be able to sit here and enjoy the view'
He said, looking out into the wilderness,
checking his watch, unable to find any part
of the crumbling bench that was comfortable.

Advice offered, that taking charge
of the fierce growth, removing the cheeky weeds,
short back and sides to the punk grass,
lining the shrubs up in single file
as though in a show of military order
they could salute me as I march through.

Paradise, an old Persian word
for a walled garden, As though
by taking control of what grows
we might create our heaven.

But I am not sure. Why
cannot we just sit and look
and find our peace in the chaos
and absence of geometry.
Once we begin to control
the growth of another,
when does it stop?

And why do we never mention
that gardens were originally
designed to show off
the fact we didn't need
to grow vegetables?

Symbiosis

I wonder if they know
what it is they do
as they multiply fast,
making a home in lung,
bladder or other organ
and inviting others in.

Do they notice where
they are, as they ride
the underground flow of blood
to establish new citadels
from which to thrive.

Do they appreciate
that life for them,
whether in balance or not,
has the power to mean
death of an unknown other?

Or like all of us, do they
simply live as their nature
demands, only understanding
what is in front of them
but totally unaware
as to what do they belong?

Wa-hu

Eyes on the peak, heart pumping,
the pack on my back is heavy but
worthy. I am alone but for the trees.
The blue sky burns, my clothes damp
and I have no troubles but to climb.

Wa-hu, I hear its deep guttural roar
echo across the valley bite into my chest.
Wa-hu, it penetrates my being, shaking
my insides long after the air falls silent.
I am not alone, none of us are.

Surrounded by scrub that is head high,
I cannot see. Repeating barks thud close,
then drift away. An unsighted mind loves
to paint, these pictures grip me deep.
Danger, the growling dawn chorus of life.

Where do the watched run? Back no better
than forward. This land is alive, just
as I am. Hunger will decide the outcome.
Unknown energy pulses heavy limbs.
Finally I am away, safe again to stride

with permission to return to the familiar
concrete, straight lines and timetable. Safe
to return my wild life to the electric cage.
Safe for however long, from having to chew on
the bones of where we all first sprung.

Sing

Let your words
be like the birds,
let them rejoice up
and fly away.

For the air
is where
they long to be,
to dance, flit and play.

Let your actions
be like the fractions,
part of much
bigger scheme.

Knowing that you
do not exist alone
despite what they
would have you dream.

For time is short,
precious and fraught,
nothing gained
by hanging on.

So open up your eyes,
heart and mouth
and rejoin the eternal choir
of creations great song

Solo

The world left me
as the sun went,
sitting quietly alone in
the advancing darkness.

Nowhere
to run,
the obscurity
cloaked it all.

Yet in the still,
lilted a soft singing
from where
I knew not.

Vibrations building
in my chest, pulsing
out to the five corners
of my own star.

A sweet wordless voice
that attempted no answer
but simply rejoiced
in its chance to sing.

Breaking

The sun rises
and the day begins,
at least it does
for me.

Somewhere else
and for someone else
the light fades
back to dark.

What to do with this
one precious moment
that exists for us all?

Are we born into life,
or by being delivered
are we in fact cut off
from the previous Eden
of an unaware totality?

Each time the day breaks,
a moment to start again.
All wounds we carry
exist only now in memories
that may not be honest.

Can we take this chance
to live, as perhaps was
the original intention?

Ride on Time

So the wheels turn, the road winds and the legs burn.
Pot holes like ragged ulcers line the sides, impatient
heavy metallic four wheelers rev and roar behind,
I wonder if they realise that they might only be slowed
down by a minute at the most in their suffering.

An ache in the neck and in the mind, remembering
previous victories and speeds that the legs cannot
give today. Previous success comes with a hidden price
that no one wants to discuss. What goes up must
come down. Not many talk about the coming down.

Alone on the road, too easy to give in to the ghosts
of previous lives, that ride effortlessly alongside.
Memory rewards and flogs in equal measure. Thoughts
flash of how it once was, only making the now harder.
Temptation to spend the whole life cycling backwards.

Fields of deep yellow rape adorn the nearby fields, fresh
vibrant and bulging life. Gentle blossom explodes on
tree after tree, the air feels alive with smell of a world
that knows it is safe to live again. Does she remember
the fruits of last year or simply decide to grow again?

Too easy to miss the chance to regenerate if we make
our efforts in pursuit of someone no longer there.
I can only ride at this moment as I can, that in itself
is something. One day I won't be able to do this,
and then I'll wonder why I spent so long wishing
that when I could, I should have been so much better.

Vicious Cycles

Because I am so angry,
my inner storms numb me
from the soft breeze
that caresses my hard face.

Because I am so angry,
the raging voices inside telling
me to destroy this and that
deafen me to the gentle wind
playing harmonies in the trees.

Because I am so angry,
I can no longer see who I am with,
but only a sea of molten fiery
objects covered in hot lava
from the exploding volcano within.

And because I am so angry,
despite any protested righteousness,
I am currently not part
of anything or anyone

but my shrinking self,
which, if I am not careful,
will only make me even
more angry than I already am!

Ditty

Where is there
when full of care?
What of here
if full of fear?

Alive we still are,
whether here or there,
so easy to forget
when seeking fancy's lair.

It matters not
when building a 'me,'
if the fretful mind
only knows to flee.

For in that place
we still shall be
despite how it seems
and no less free.

Everything we need
awaits us where we stand,
nothing we seek anywhere else
despite yet another
fearful ego demand.

Embers

Millions of sunsets, drifting
from stretching branches. Dying
embers from creation's hot flame
floating down to deep roots.

Falling silently to a softening earth,
weaving a fleeting golden carpet
for existence to rustle its gentle way
forward to a hungry wintery sleep.

Growth becomes malignant
unless there is rest. Look
around. What truly lives
that does not how to breath?

Come home, the invisible calls
to those who desired to be made.
Come back to where you began.
So when ready, you can give again.

There, There

'We're getting there,'
the old man rumbled.
His grey pallor indistinguishable
from the low heavy cloud
that surrounded them.

'And when we are there,'
his young accomplice begun.
Whose soft face
had already begun to crease
from always thinking
about the unmade yesterdays
and the promise of tomorrow's arrival.
'Will that be when we can finally stop moving?'

'Unlikely,' the old man sighed,
squinting at the dull horizon,
and trudging forward.

His young companion, knowing
no better, simply followed his grey guide
along the crumbling road
that never seemed to end.
Preferring any sort of company
than having to be alone.

Red Lights on the Cycle Home

Red light as the rain pours,
still so far to go, just to
get to work. The lives of
others live both behind
and lie waiting in front.

A time to pause, feel the
water soak into my fibres.
Feel my feet lose their feeling.
We make our choices.
Mine to make today harder
than it ever had to be.

But I wouldn't be anywhere
else, waiting for the lights
to change. The pulsing Wye
swaggers the opposite way
that I have chosen to go.

Soft light illuminates the valley.
A curved palette of greens,
blues and browns hold
the stage, while naked branches
click and clack as the wind drifts.

There is only ever here, no
matter where I find myself.
A place of endless change
and possibility. Right now

I am in *this* here, waiting for the lights
to change. Cold, expectant, with
somewhere meaningful awaiting
my arrival. And it is glorious.

Other Titles by Giles Dawnay

Dancing Shadows
Beyond the Falling
12 Labors of Hippocrates
Brushstrokes – reflections on illness
Go Gently into the Day
Begin Again

Coming soon – first novel
The Rising of the Son

www.gilesdawnaypoetry.com

Title Cover Artwork by Amy Dawnay

Environmentally Conscious Artist and Illustrator

www.amydawnay.com

38758060R00050

Printed in Great Britain
by Amazon